WASTE AND RECYCLING

Barbara James

Also in paperback:

Acid Rain
Conserving the Atmosphere
Conserving the Polar Regions
Conserving Rainforests
Farming and the Environment
Protecting the Oceans
Protecting Wildlife
The Spread of Deserts

Cover: A tail-back of disused cars at a
dump in the USA.

Series editor: Sue Hadden
Series designer: Ross George

First published in 1989 by
Wayland (Publishers) Ltd
61 Western Road, Hove
East Sussex BN3 1JD, England

This edition published in 1991 by
Wayland (Publishers) Ltd

**British Library Cataloguing in
Publication Data**
James, Barbara
    Waste recycling.
    1. Recycling (Waste, etc.)
    I. Title   II. Series
    604.6

ISBN 0-7502-0274-2

Typeset by L. George and R. Gibbs, Wayland.
Printed in Italy by G. Canale C.S.p.A., Turin
Bound in Belgium by Casterman S.A.

Contents

Introduction

The voyage of the Karin B

In late August 1988 the *Karin B*, a West German freighter, was anchored off the Cornish coast in Britain. A Royal Navy vessel was standing guard. The Captain of the *Karin B* was hoping to end his two-month voyage around the seas looking for a port that would let his ship dock – with its cargo. The *Karin B* had already been refused entry in Italy, Germany and Spain because she was carrying 167 containers holding 2,000 tonnes of poisonous waste chemicals.

This toxic waste itself was well-travelled. It is

In August 1988 the Karin B toured European ports in search of one that would accept its cargo of toxic waste. Eventually, it was forced to return to Italy from where it had started its long journey.

uncertain where it was originally produced but it was dumped illegally in Nigeria by an Italian company. When Nigeria ordered its removal, the *Karin B* was hired to pick up the deadly cargo and return it to Italy. However, the Italian authorities refused entry to their port and so began the voyage of the *Karin B*.

In Britain, the Government was under intense pressure from the public and the press to stop the ship entering Plymouth harbour. Permission to dock was refused and the *Karin B* set off again. The Captain, Richard Hinterleitner said, 'I don't think I'll be handling toxic waste again'.

The *Karin B's* voyage is short compared to those of the barges *Khian Sea* and *Bark*. They have been at sea for eighteen months looking for somewhere to dump their cargoes of stinking sewage. They have sailed from the USA, where the sewage originated, to the Caribbean in their search for a port that will accept them.

These three ships and many more are carrying the waste that nobody wants. Not all waste is so difficult to dispose of, or so deadly, but the disposal of waste is a 'hot' environmental issue because of the way it can affect our planet. In this book we shall look at the different types of waste, how they are dealt with and the effects that waste can have on the earth's natural cycles. The waste story is not all gloom and doom – refuse, reclamation and recycling are vital alternative methods of handling waste and this book will look at some schemes in operation. It will also give you some ideas about what you can do to reduce, re-use and recycle waste.

Greenpeace, an environmental pressure group, aims to influence public and political opinion by non-violent campaigning. It has publicized environmental issues, such as the pollution of the North Sea from sewage, and industrial and domestic waste.

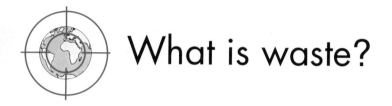

What is waste?

Nature and waste

What happens to wild birds and animals when they die? Where do all the leaves go once they have fallen in autumn? They are dealt with by nature's recycling system. All dead plants and animals decay and decompose. They are broken down by maggots, worms, bacteria and fungi and so the chemicals and nutrients they contain return to the earth. They may go into the soil, the sea or perhaps a river, where they are used again by growing plants and animals. This is a natural process in which waste materials are re-used. It is a never-ending cycle of death, decay, new life and growth.

A good example of this cycle is a garden compost heap. Compost heaps are valuable because they rot down garden waste, as well as vegetable peelings and waste food, and produce humus. Humus is dug back into the soil where it aids new growth and improves the structure and texture of the soil.

Nature is very efficient at dealing with waste. In fact, it is not really waste because it is used again and becomes a resource. A dead tree trunk

*The diagram **below** shows a woodland recycling system. All healthy habitats have such cycles but when they become polluted, the cycles are in danger of breaking down.*

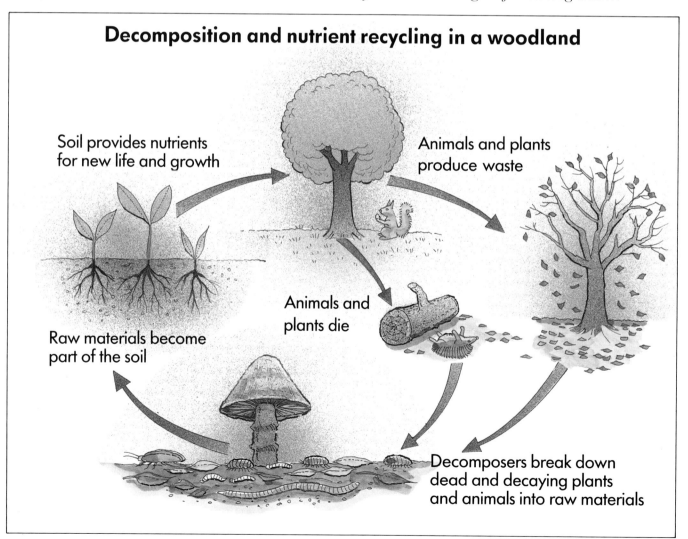

Decomposition and nutrient recycling in a woodland

Soil provides nutrients for new life and growth

Animals and plants produce waste

Animals and plants die

Raw materials become part of the soil

Decomposers break down dead and decaying plants and animals into raw materials

A mountain of unwanted cars in the USA. Unlike many consumer products, cars are usually recycled for their scrap metal.

A dead tree trunk is a valuable resource for this American pileated woodpecker, which is using it for a nest hole.

becomes a home for insects and birds, such as woodpeckers, before it eventually rots down into the earth to become humus. On the rocks of the west coast of South America are huge colonies of fish-eating birds. Their droppings are rich in the mineral phosphorous which encourages plants to grow. These enormous deposits of bird droppings, or 'guano', have been used as an agricultural fertilizer by humans. So what is waste to one species is a resource to another.

While nature is very good at re-use and recycling, humans can be very efficient at wasting materials. In one day the USA disposes of 90 million bottles and jars; 46 million cans and 25,000 television sets. Although some of these resources are used again, most of them are dumped as rubbish. As more and more rubbish accumulates, the demand for holes in the ground, landfill sites, in which to deposit waste has grown rapidly. Human waste may travel many kilometres before it is finally dumped – domestic waste from London is transported to landfill sites in seven British counties.

Many waste products do not decompose easily. Here in Manitoba, Canada, polar bears are foraging for food on a garbage dump.

The earth's natural cycles of decomposition and recycling can cope with some human waste. However the huge amount of waste that humans throw away is overloading the system. The problem is made worse because many of the substances manufactured by humans are not biodegradable. This means that they do not decompose easily. Glass, tin and some plastics are not biodegradable and they take many years to break down. Waste materials which are dumped and do not decompose quickly may cause pollution.

Pollution

When humans are wasteful with the earth's resources and do not re-use or recycle materials, the environment becomes polluted with waste products. Pollution prevents the earth's natural cycles from working properly. It is also unsightly and often dangerous.

Polluted environments are a health hazard – they threaten the health of our planet, as well as our own lives. If domestic waste is not taken away from our homes, there would soon be mounds of rotting waste which would attract flies and rats. Although these animals perform a useful function in helping to decompose waste, they can also carry disease which is deadly to humans. Similarly, if factories are allowed to continue to pour chemical waste into rivers and seas, the planet's water will become poisoned.

The unique planet

The Earth is the only known planet to support life. It has all the resources and materials to enable plants and animals, including humans, to survive. The Earth provides water, air, energy, food, minerals, metals and medicines, as well as recycling systems so that the resources are re-used. It also supports our quality of life – arts, sciences, recreation and religious beliefs.

These resources and materials, however, are limited and need to be used wisely and conserved. The Earth's natural systems are vital to life but they will break down if they are overloaded. The survival and well-being of life on Earth is linked to the environment. Our own lives and those of future generations depend on us treating the Earth with care and respect.

Domestic waste

The consumer society

We live in a society that consumes, or uses, many resources. It is often called 'the consumer society' and this usually refers to Western countries including Europe, the USA and Canada, Japan, Australia and New Zealand. These countries have developed lifestyles which use many products such as cars, televisions, furniture, refrigerators, books and cosmetics. Lifestyles like these consume many of the world's resources.

These societies have not always used so much. During the Second World War materials and resources were scarce because trading systems did not, or could not, operate. Countries had to introduce rationing of food and other necessities such as petrol, and people were encouraged to conserve and recycle materials. For example, many women re-used fabric from old dresses to make new ones.

Many of the world's resources are used to enable the consumer society to have labour-saving devices. How many kitchen gadgets do you use in your home?

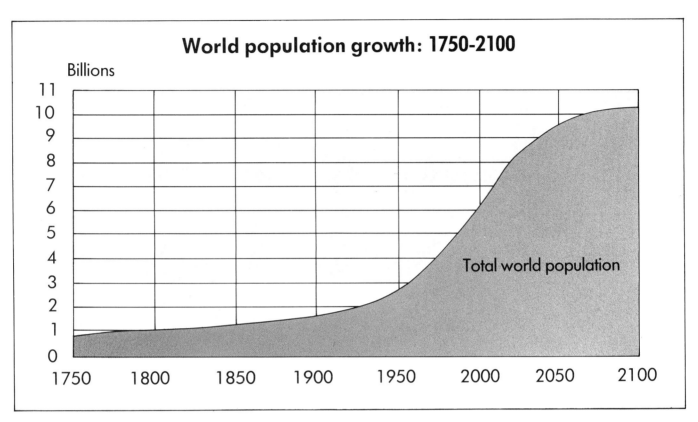

World population growth: 1750-2100

Billions

*The **above** graph shows the rise in the world's population since 1750 and the predicted population for the year 2000.*

Right *One third of the world's population uses over 80% of the world's resources. The remaining 20% is used by the rest of the world.*

In the years since the Second World War, the world population has increased dramatically. Cities have become larger because, throughout the world, there is a trend towards urbanization. This means that people leave rural communities to seek a living in the city. City-dwellers, particularly in Western countries, require food and goods to be brought into the city. They wish to have convenience foods and luxury items, such as freezers and videocassette players. They use and throw away large amounts of materials, especially packaging. In a city environment, natural recycling systems cannot operate. There is too much waste for them to cope with.

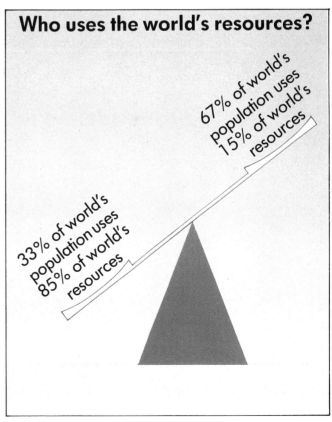

Who uses the world's resources?

67% of world's population uses 15% of world's resources

33% of world's population uses 85% of world's resources

Throwing it away

Look at what *you* throw away each day. Drink cans, sweet wrappers, leftover food, paper and bottles are just some of the items to be found in a typical dustbin. You may think this is all rubbish but they are valuable resources – paper, glass, plastic, metal.

Much of the contents of a dustbin is packaging. The cardboard, paper and plastic containers surrounding a product are designed to make it more attractive to the buyer, but all this packaging

In many countries, people make their living by re-using other people's waste. The photograph shows a waste tip in the Philippines.

*You can see from the illustration **below** how much packaging surrounds a few chocolates.*

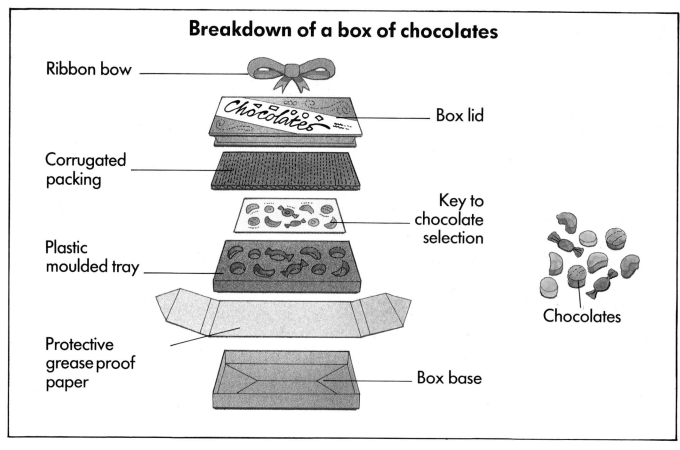

Breakdown of a box of chocolates

Ribbon bow

Box lid

Corrugated packing

Key to chocolate selection

Plastic moulded tray

Chocolates

Protective grease proof paper

Box base

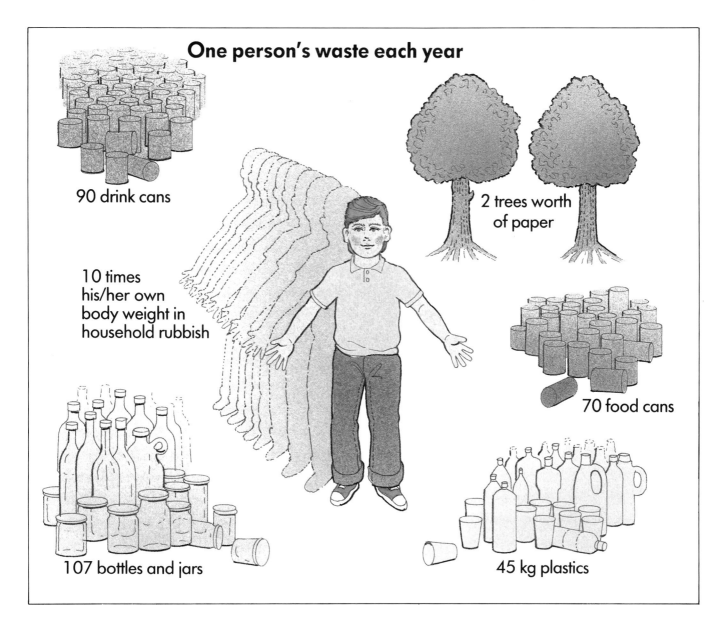

One person's waste each year

90 drink cans

10 times his/her own body weight in household rubbish

2 trees worth of paper

70 food cans

107 bottles and jars

45 kg plastics

*The diagram **above** illustrates the average amount of waste produced by one person in one year.*

is thrown away. Paper and card form two-thirds of the waste from people's homes.

The packaging story is not all bad news, however. Some packaging is necessary to keep products such as food clean and free from contamination. Also, more and more packages are being made from recycled materials. For example, cardboard is made from recycled paper.

Waste management

Because there is so much domestic waste, we have had to devise ways to dispose of it. In Europe each household fills, on average, two dustbins a week. Multiply this by the number of households in an entire country and you have a huge amount of waste to be dealt with. The city of New York in the USA throws out the most waste per person per day – approximately 1.8 kg per person. Every day New York has to dispose of 24,000 tonnes of waste.

So what happens to the waste we put into our dustbins? First it is collected, by the local authority, or a private company, and taken to a rubbish tip, along with waste from the other homes in the area. At the tip some sorting of the waste may be done – scrap metal is often taken out to be melted down and re-used. What happens to the waste then varies from place to place. In general, the most popular solution to the waste mountain is to bury it in landfill sites. Britain disposes of about 90 per cent of its waste in this way.

There are problems with landfill sites, however. The decaying waste produces gases (mainly methane) which seep up through the ground. Occasionally, these gases have caused

Collection of domestic waste is vital to the health of the community. Refuse collectors (**inset photograph**) *take the waste to a rubbish tip, such as this one in Japan.*

explosions or entailed buildings erected on the site to be evacuated. The buried waste can also pollute the ground water. This runs into rivers and streams which supply our drinking water.

Another method of disposal is incineration, or burning the waste. This method is becoming more popular as landfill sites are becoming scarce and, therefore, more expensive. An advantage of incineration is that energy can be produced from the burning waste, and there are now some 'energy from waste' schemes in operation. This is particularly popular in Denmark, where 75 per cent of its waste is burnt to produce energy. There are also drawbacks to this system of disposal. It costs a great deal of money to develop incineration systems. More seriously, the gases emitted during the burning process pollute the air.

Waste is expensive – it costs time, energy and space, as well as money. Britain pays £1 million a day to dispose of waste into landfill sites. It is estimated that California, USA, will have to pay $1 billion a year by the 1990s to dispose of its waste. Not only does waste cost a lot of money, it can also pollute the environment. However rubbish does not need to be wasted. It can be *re-used* and *recycled*.

Another method of waste disposal is incineration, or burning. Energy can be produced as a by-product but air pollution can be a problem.

Re-use and recycling

We can see examples of re-use and recycling all around us. The clothing, toys and books passed on to friends, relatives or charity shops are being re-used. In many areas local authorities, or sometimes voluntary groups, have set up recycling schemes such as bottle banks, tin banks or waste paper collections, where local people can take their rubbish. City authorities are looking more and more at recycling schemes because this form of waste management saves money, resources and energy.

Recycling can also be less damaging to the environment. Paper recycling not only saves the trees that are felled to make paper, but it also reduces air and water pollution and conserves valuable energy.

Bottle banks are becoming a common feature of city life. You can help the environment by saving your glass bottles and taking them to be recycled.

The Oregon Example

The state of Oregon in the USA shows what can be done if there is political and popular support. Oregon has a law, the Recycling Opportunity Act, to make recycling available to all its citizens. The Act aims to:

- reduce the amount of waste generated
- re-use materials where possible
- recycle non-reusable materials
- use waste that cannot be re-used or recycled in 'energy from waste' schemes
- dispose of the remaining waste by landfilling or other appropriate methods

Oregon doesn't stop there. It also reduces the taxes paid by businesses involved in recycling schemes.

Above *and* **below** *These centres in London and Grenoble, France, sort and separate waste for recycling. Paper, metal and glass can be easily dealt with, but so far there has been little progress in processes to recycle plastics.*

Industrial waste

Domestic waste is only a small part of the total waste produced. Industry is also responsible for large amounts of waste – coal mining tips, slag heaps, chemical waste, and the gas and smoke that pour out of factory chimneys.

Industrialized societies need industry to produce the energy and goods that the population expect to maintain their lifestyle. Industries include food processing, mining, petro-chemical and plastic production, metals and chemicals, paper and pulp, and the manufacture of consumer goods like televisions. In turn, industry depends on the raw materials such as iron, water and wood to manufacture goods. This manufacturing process produces waste products and, while some of these industrial wastes are relatively harmless, others are highly toxic. The toxic wastes can do great harm to nature and to humans, particularly as they are produced in such large quantities.

The tall chimneys of power stations emit sulphur dioxide, which can drift in the air above crop fields.

Hazardous waste

About 10 to 20 per cent of industrial waste could be dangerous to humans and to natural systems. Hazardous waste includes chemicals like cyanide, pesticides such as DDT, solvents, asbestos and metals such as mercury and cadmium. Industry disposes of this dangerous waste in a variety of ways. Some waste, particularly solid waste, is dumped in landfill sites, while liquid waste is often pumped into rivers or the sea. Ninety per cent of waste ends up in the sea one way or another.

Some hazardous wastes are dumped into the environment precisely because they are so dangerous. It is not known how to deal with them safely and it is hoped that the environment can absorb the toxic substances. However, this is not a safe solution to the problem. Many metals and chemicals are not natural and are not biodegradable. Therefore, as more and more waste is dumped, the earth's natural cycles are threatened and the environment becomes polluted. Since the 1950s chemical and toxic waste pollution disasters have become more common and more serious.

A photograph taken by Greenpeace campaigners. It shows toxic waste called yellow sludge being dumped off the coast of northern France. Every day, a French chemicals company dumps 2,000 tonnes of this yellow sludge into the Channel.

Waste disasters

1959	Minimata, Japan	Mercury is discharged into waterways. 400 dead; 2,000 injured.
1974	Flixborough, UK	An explosion at a chemical plant. 23 dead; 104 injured; 3,000 evacuated.
1976	Seveso, Italy	Leakage of dioxin. 193 injured; 730 evacuated.
1978	Manfredonia, Italy	Ammonia is released from chemical plant. 10,000 evacuated.
1984	Bhopal, India	Leakage of pesticide from factory. 2,500 dead; thousands injured; 200,000 evacuated.

(Information from UNEP)

At present there are more than seven million known chemicals, and thousands of new ones are discovered every year. As more chemicals are discovered, it becomes even more difficult to deal with the wastes effectively.

Pollution knows no frontiers

Hazardous waste may be produced in one country, but when it is pumped into a river, the sea or the atmosphere, the effects are felt in another country. In 1986, a fire at a chemical factory by the River Rhine in Switzerland resulted in serious river pollution in Germany, France and Holland which badly affected the North Sea. Wastes from power stations in Britain cause air pollution which falls as acid rain in Norway and Sweden.

Further afield, toxic substances are being found in the deep ocean trenches far away from human settlements. Antarctica, often called 'the last wilderness', has also been found to contain pollutants. The pollution has travelled across the globe from industrial nations.

Some industrial waste is so toxic that protective clothing and special equipment is needed to deal with it.

Left *In 1976 the chemical dioxin leaked from a factory in Seveso, Italy. Crops and livestock were poisoned, while many local people suffered long-term health problems.*

Below *One of the world's worst chemical disasters was at Bhopal, India in 1984. Thousands of people were killed or injured and 200,000 people were evacuated from their homes.*

The oceans

The threat to the world's seas and oceans from waste and pollution is becoming obvious. The North Sea has long been a dumping ground for waste from many European countries. Chemicals such as PCBs (polychlorinated biphenols) and pesticides such as DDT, as well as domestic waste, oil, incinerated waste and sewage, are all regularly disposed of at sea. The sea is used as a dustbin and there will have to be an international effort to clean it up.

Above *Oil pollution is a serious threat to the world's oceans and has a devastating effect on coastline habitats. This oil spill occurred in San Francisco bay, USA.*

Left *Pollution of the North Sea is widely thought to have contributed to the death of many grey seals during 1988.*

The Beluga whale – victim of toxic waste

In Canada, stocks of the white Beluga whale in the St. Lawrence Seaway are severely reduced. In 1900, 5,000 whales lived in the Seaway and now there are estimated to be 450 whales. Researchers believe that toxic waste from industrial sites along the river is causing the whales to die from blood poisoning. Examinations of their bodies have shown a very high level of harmful chemicals, including PCBs, DDT, mercury and cadmium.

The beautiful beluga, or white whale, has been called the most polluted mammal on earth.

An end to the dumping?

The toxic waste situation has become more serious with disasters occurring more frequently. At last humans have woken up to what they are doing to their planet. Environmental pressure groups such as Greenpeace and Friends of the Earth have campaigned to bring this pollution to the attention of governments and the public. As public awareness and press attention has grown, there have been moves to restrict the dumping of waste. Some regulations have been tightened but it is a slow process and alternative disposal methods have to be found.

Importing and exporting pollution

Britain has been called 'the dustbin of Europe' because it imports toxic wastes from other countries. Holland, Ireland, Belgium, the USA, Canada and many other countries pay Britain to dispose of their waste. Most of this waste is put into landfill sites but some is incinerated or treated. The United Kingdom Royal Commission on Environmental Pollution has expressed its concern over the trade in waste into Britain. It has called for improved regulations on hazardous waste treatment and disposal.

Greenpeace campaigners often attempt to stop the dumping of waste in the sea. The photograph, taken in 1982, shows six members of Greenpeace who chained themselves to a ship dumping waste in the Atlantic Ocean. Such protest actions are often effective.

As anti-pollution laws have become stricter in developed countries, industries have looked elsewhere to dispose of their waste. Many developing countries in the Third World have become a dustbin for industrial waste. A report by Greenpeace shows that waste from Europe and the USA is dumped unmonitored in many countries of Africa and South America. The United Nations Environment Programme is now working to reduce the widespread international trade in toxic waste.

Agricultural waste

Over half the total waste produced by the European Economic Community (EEC) comes from farming. This huge amount of waste is the result of changes in farming methods over the last thirty years. Traditionally animals were kept in the fields, while different crops were grown in rotation to keep the soil healthy. Farms were 'mixed', that is, they farmed both livestock and crops. Over the years, farming has become more specialized and intensive. More animals are farmed but in smaller areas and often in indoor units. Farmers can produce more food this way but the animals need more care. Their feed has to be taken to them and their waste has to be taken away. On arable farms, crops are also grown intensively and a farmer may grow wheat year after year, using fertilizer to enrich the soil rather than crop rotation.

Intensive farming involves keeping many animals in a small area, as on this farm in Australia.

Main picture *Intensively-farmed animals produce much waste, which is stored in slurry lagoons or pits. Often it leaks into the ground, polluting the groundwater. The* **inset photograph** *shows what happens when fertilizers are washed into rivers and ponds. The nitrates they contain encourage a build-up of algae, which prevents oxygen from reaching other creatures.*

Animal waste

Intensive farming involves keeping more animals which, in turn, means more dung. Australian and American cattle ranches must cope with very large quantities of dung. Britain alone has to deal with about 20 million tonnes of dung each year! Such huge amounts cannot be recycled naturally so systems have been developed to store and dispose of it. At the farm, the waste, or slurry, is kept in pits and later spread on to the fields. If it is spread too thickly the natural cycles of decomposition cannot operate. This causes some of the waste to wash off into the ground water or into rivers and streams, causing water pollution. The pits may also leak waste in to these water courses. Pollution of rivers and streams is increasing and many incidents are linked to agricultural practices.

The pollution of rivers and streams by organic waste can threaten the life cycles in the water. Waste entering the water is gradually broken down by micro-organisms, but these use up much oxygen when dealing with the pollutants. This can result in not enough oxygen being left for other life, such as fish and plants.

Fertilizers

Modern arable farmers use chemical fertilizers containing nitrogen to improve plant growth and increase food production. All plants need minerals such as potassium, nitrogen and phosphorus for growth. A healthy soil can provide these but artificial fertilizers add more. The nitrogen in the fertilizer is broken down by the soil to produce nitrates which are taken up by plants. Too much fertilizer produces too many nitrates and some are not absorbed by plants. Instead they are washed by rain from the soil into the ground water or into rivers. Again, the waters are polluted but this time by nitrates.

Water in rivers and streams is used to supply drinking water and there is now concern over the high levels of nitrates in tap water. Pollution of water supplies by nitrates is thought to be linked to various illnesses including stomach cancer and 'blue baby syndrome'. The EEC has set standards for nitrate levels in European drinking water but they are not always met. In 1987, the Yorkshire Water Authority in Britain had to deliver bottled water for some new-born babies because the nitrate levels in the tap water were too high.

The diagram shows the water cycle and also shows how organic waste and fertilizers pollute the water.

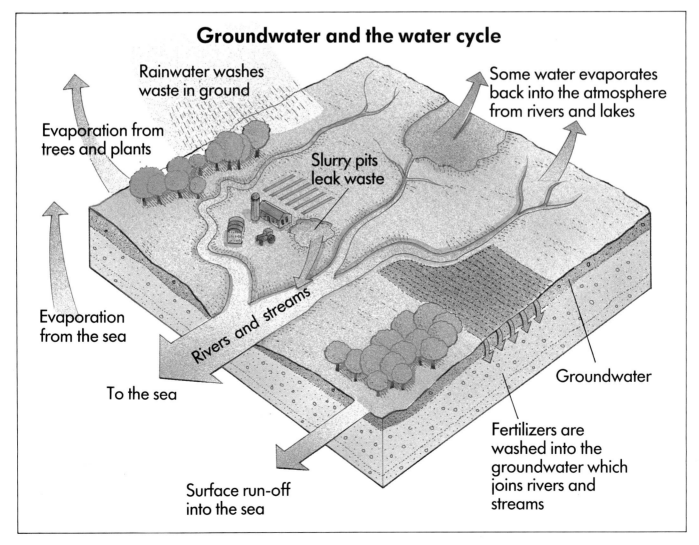

Groundwater and the water cycle

Rainwater washes waste in ground

Some water evaporates back into the atmosphere from rivers and lakes

Evaporation from trees and plants

Slurry pits leak waste

Evaporation from the sea

Rivers and streams

To the sea

Groundwater

Surface run-off into the sea

Fertilizers are washed into the groundwater which joins rivers and streams

Surplus farm produce

In many western countries, farming has become so efficient that there are surpluses. Within the European Community, there are 'mountains' of surplus grain, and 'lakes' of milk and wine. To keep prices high, the surpluses are stored or destroyed. In the USA, the government buys surplus milk, grain and meat in order to keep prices high and more farmers in business. Without these purchases, thousands of farmers would go out of business, causing food prices to rise even further.

Every year, the American government sells cheaply or gives away tonnes of farm products to food banks and schools. In 1984, for example, it gave away 5 million kilos of cheese per month.

In the USA, the government buys millions of kilos of food for use in school lunches, so using up some surplus food.

Each farmer in the USA produces enough wheat for 70 people in the world.

Radioactive waste

What is radioactivity?

In 1896, a French scientist Antoine Becquerel was studying the element uranium. By chance, he placed the uranium close to a photographic plate and, when looking at the plate some time later, he saw unusual dark marks upon it. The uranium was giving out, or emitting, particles (or 'rays') which were affecting the plate. This was the discovery of radiation.

Radiation is emitted by many other elements as well as uranium – radium, potassium, thorium, carbon and iodine are just a few. These elements are said to be radioactive. All radiation can be harmful to humans and other animals because it can damage living cells. The greater the amount of radiation, the greater the possibility of damage. People have used this characteristic of radiation to treat some illnesses, such as cancer. A certain dose of radiation is given to the patient to kill cancerous body cells.

Radioactive materials are used in agriculture, industry, medicine, scientific research and engineering, as well as in the production of nuclear power and nuclear weapons. All these processes produce wastes which are radioactive and have to be disposed of. Although all radioactivity decays (or fades) with time, it takes some radioactive materials many millions of years to do so. It is important, therefore, that waste is stored safely if it is not to harm the present and future generations of life on earth.

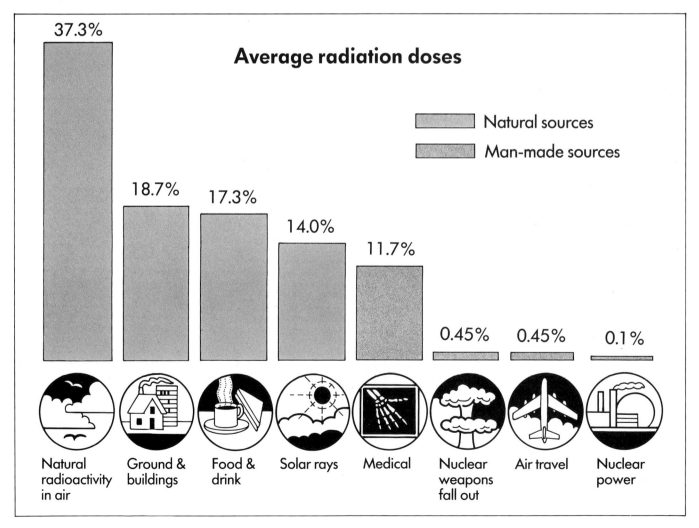

Average radiation doses

Natural sources
Man-made sources

Natural radioactivity in air	Ground & buildings	Food & drink	Solar rays	Medical	Nuclear weapons fall out	Air travel	Nuclear power
37.3%	18.7%	17.3%	14.0%	11.7%	0.45%	0.45%	0.1%

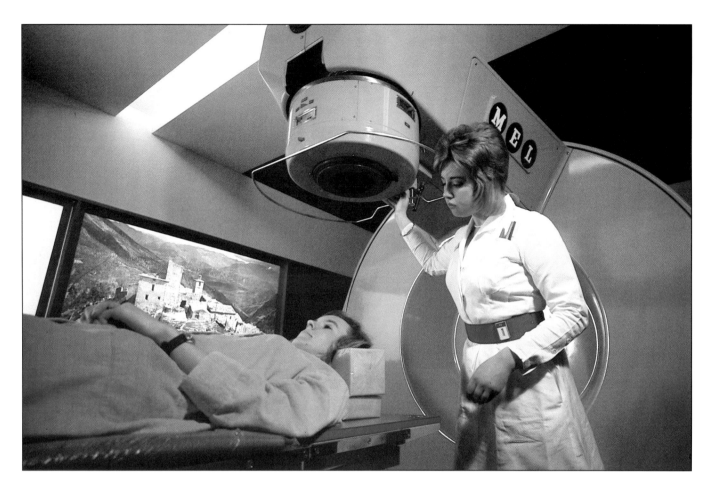

Above *Radiation can be used to treat many forms of cancer.*

The diagram **opposite** *illustrates average radiation doses from natural and man-made sources. You can see that natural radioactivity in the air accounts for most of it.*

Low-level waste

This is short-lived waste which has a low radioactive content. It includes contaminated protective clothing and some equipment from hospitals, factories, universities and from the nuclear power industry.

Disposal methods: in trenches in the ground; dumped at sea in steel drums (this is no longer allowed in some countries); some liquid wastes are pumped into the sea, and waste gases are discharged into the atmosphere.

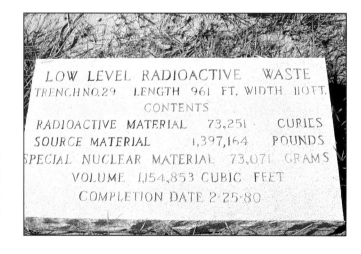

Low-level radioactive waste is often buried in the ground. This marker provides some information about the type and amount of waste buried at a site in the USA.

Intermediate-level waste

Includes bulkier solid wastes such as used equipment, transportation flasks and radioactive sludges from power stations, fuel reprocessing plants and nuclear weapons establishments.

Disposal methods: encased in concrete and stored at special sites, usually at nuclear power stations. Researchers are looking into methods of disposal in deep underground sites or underneath the sea bed.

High-level waste

Highly radioactive waste includes used fuel rods and liquid waste from the nuclear power industry. It has to be kept cool.

Disposal methods: liquids are stored in stainless steel tanks surrounded by concrete at special sites; they can also be solidified in glass and stored in steel containers in concrete vaults or deep underground. Researchers are also looking at ocean bed disposal.

Above *In October 1988 German Greenpeace campaigners protested against the dumping of Swedish nuclear waste in their country. Greenpeace have also successfully stopped the dumping of radioactive waste in the Atlantic Ocean.*

Opposite *These drums of radioactive waste are being transported to a special disposal site. Strict security and safety measures are necessary, including encasing the waste in concrete and steel.*

How to dispose of radioactive wastes safely is a controversial issue. Many people are worried by radioactivity, especially as it cannot be seen, touched, smelt or tasted. A large number of local groups have campaigned against the disposal of waste in their area. Environmental pressure groups have also undertaken long campaigns to stop the dumping of radioactive waste. In 1983 a successful Greenpeace campaign led to the end of dumping in the Atlantic Ocean. In 1984 Greenpeace campaigners temporarily blocked the pipes pumping liquid radioactive waste from the Sellafield nuclear plant into the Irish Sea.

Nuclear power and radioactivity - the risks

To light and heat houses, cook food, travel, and provide power for industry, large amounts of electrical energy are needed. In developed countries, electricity is readily available in most homes, offices and factories and it is generated at power stations using coal, oil and nuclear energy.

All energy production produces waste and involves risks to humans and the environment. Coal-mining waste is piled up into heaps; there are pit disasters which kill miners; and the coal power stations' waste gases contribute to the acid rain problem. Oil rigs burn off waste gas and oil, and oil-exploration disasters, like the Piper Alpha explosion in 1988, can occur.

While an adequate supply of electrical power is essential to the modern world, the various types of energy must be carefully examined. Above all, the risks to human and environmental health have to be taken into account.

In July 1988, an explosion at the Piper Alpha oil rig in the North Sea killed 167 people.

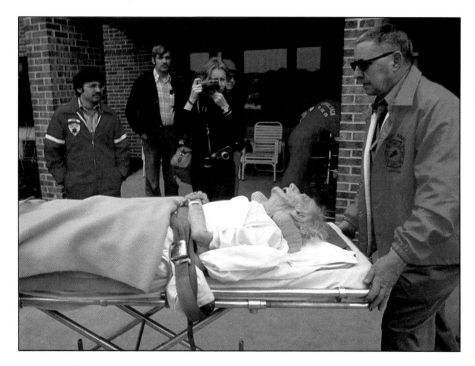

The nuclear accident at Three Mile Island, in 1979, resulted in the evacuation of many people from their homes.

Nuclear power is an important source of energy but its waste products are dangerous. Apart from the problem of radioactive waste, there have been several major nuclear accidents. In 1957, a fire at Windscale in Britain resulted in radioactive contamination of surrounding farmland. In 1979 at Three Mile Island, USA, an accident in the nuclear reactor contaminated the site and cost $1 billion to clean up.

The most serious nuclear accident occurred at the Chernobyl power station in the USSR in 1986. An explosion and fire sent radioactive materials into the surrounding area, which entailed the evacuation of towns and villages. The area is highly radioactive and will remain so for many years. The radioactive particles, called 'fall-out', were carried by winds to other countries, including Sweden, Germany and Britain. Even several years later, land and grass in some areas of Britain are still radioactive, with the result that sheep grazing there become radioactive and are unfit to be eaten by humans. Worst affected of all were the reindeer herds and the Lapp people in northern Sweden. The animals and some of the herders are still highly radioactive.

In the USSR strawberries are tested for their radiation levels, following the 1986 explosion at the Chernobyl nuclear power station.

Sewage

What goes down the sink, the drain and the toilet is called sewage and it is one of the biggest sources of waste. In most areas, to protect public health, sewage is collected in sewers and drains leading to a sewage treatment plant. The wastes are separated here, with the liquids being cleaned and returned to the river. The solids are processed to form 'sludge' which is disposed of on the land or in the sea. The gases given off by the sewage can be used to produce electricity to run the treatment plant.

Many towns, however, still pour sewage untreated into rivers or the sea. At the coastline, beaches and the sea can become so seriously polluted that swimming is unsafe because of the health risks. If it is unhealthy for humans, it must harm the plants and animals whose home it is.

Above *Marine life can be poisoned by the wastes dumped at sea. The lumps on this fish are likely to have been caused by toxic waste.*

Below *This beach at San Francisco, USA, was closed because of the high levels of sewage waste.*

WARNING
SEWAGE DISCHARGE
DO NOT USE
BEACH OR WATER
S.F. DEPT. PUBLIC HEALTH

Medical waste

Hospitals and clinics have waste products to be disposed of which may be infectious or contaminated. They also must dispose of waste drugs and medicines which could be harmful to the wrong person. In addition, hospitals produce a large amount of ordinary waste and this is disposed of in the same way as normal domestic waste. Contaminated hospital waste is usually incinerated on the site but in 1988 beaches in New York and New Jersey, USA, were closed after the discovery of dangerous hospital waste washed up on them. The New York City Health

A beach at Coney Island, USA, lies deserted. Dangerous medical waste, including infected syringes, has been washed up on such beaches, after being illegally dumped in the sea. This creates a major public health risk.

Department suspect that the waste was dumped in the sea illegally, but the incident highlights the problem of unlawful dumping and the need to dispose of contaminated waste safely.

If you have waste drugs or medicines at home, you should not burn them or flush them away. They should always be returned to the chemist or pharmacist, who can dispose of them safely.

Vehicle exhausts

The waste gases from cars pollute the environment and can harm people's health. Vehicle exhaust pipes are responsible for producing most of the carbon monoxide and lead in the air, as well as being a major contributor to the acid rain problem. Lead is highly toxic and can be very damaging to children and unborn babies. To create a safer environment, lead-free petrol is now being promoted in many countries. Exhaust gases also contain hydrocarbons and nitrogen oxides which contribute to smog, a form of air pollution. The famous Los Angeles smogs are largely due to the exhaust fumes from cars.

Catalytic converters are being increasingly used to control exhaust gases. When fitted to a car, they convert the harmful gases into water vapour and carbon dioxide, but they can only be used with unleaded petrol. Another potential solution to vehicle exhaust pollution is the 'lean-burn' engine, which is being developed by

Above *Exhaust fumes from vehicles are harmful to human health and the environment.*

Below *This man's car is converted to run on methane gas produced from manure.*

By using public transport, such as buses or trains, we can reduce the stress on the environment from vehicle exhaust fumes. These articulated Canadian buses can carry many passengers.

vehicle manufacturers. Such engines burn fuel more efficiently, so reducing waste and pollution.

Another way of reducing waste and pollution from vehicles is to use them less frequently. If you look at the morning traffic jam into a city, you will see many cars with only one person sitting in them. Each car is using valuable energy and producing unpleasant waste. Using bicycles, buses, trains or sharing cars are easy ways of helping the environment.

Litter

An everyday form of waste is litter. Litter is not just the sweet papers, bus tickets and drink cans that are thrown away, but also includes old cars that have been dumped, bottles, discarded fishing tackle and plastic bags. Litter is any waste that has not been disposed of properly. It is another form of pollution.

Litter is found on city streets, in country lanes and on beaches. It is usually unpleasant and ugly. It can also be dangerous – cigarette ends can cause fires, bottles can be death-traps for small mammals such as mice and voles, and plastic bags can choke grazing animals.

Think about what you throw away. How do you feel about litter in your local area?

A moorhen is freed after becoming entangled in fishing line thrown away by an angler.

Cleaning up

'The best thing that can be said about the state of the world environment today is that people all over the world have started to worry about it' (United Nations Environment Programme News).

The statement in this report from the United Nations Environment Programme may seem gloomy, but it is a sign that changes are under way. Humans have begun to realize how they have threatened 'Mother Earth' by the careless use of her resources, by pollution and by a disregard for her delicate natural cycles. They have also begun to see that their own health and enjoyment of life depends on a healthy environment, and that good environmental practice saves money in the long-term. There is still much work to be done to restore the earth's natural balance, but there are some encouraging developments.

Some children taking part in a voluntary scheme to clean and restore an overgrown, polluted lake. The lake had to be cleared, drained and lined with new clay. Such restored lakes gradually become repopulated with water plants and animals.

Pressure groups and public opinion

As the state of the world environment has worsened, pressure groups have set up and campaigned to bring the situation to the attention of the public and of governments. There are now many pressure groups worldwide who are working to improve the environment. They are not just working to reduce levels of waste and pollution, but are also involved in protecting endangered wildlife and habitats, conserving energy, and improving city life, transport, and education. This is called the Green Movement and it is growing rapidly.

There has been an 'information explosion' on environmental issues. Accurate and up-to-date

As environmental issues have hit the headlines more frequently, the Green movement has become increasingly popular, especially in West Germany and the Netherlands. Pictured above is Petra Kelly, leader of the German political party, die Grünen.

information is essential to monitor the state of the world and to educate and inform people. Environmental information is becoming more widely available through books, magazines, newspapers, and radio and television programmes. Now an increasing number of interested and concerned people are joining together to discuss environmental problems from local meetings to international conferences.

In Britain, government plans to establish new dumps for radioactive waste were abandoned after local people mounted vigorous campaigns to protect their environment.

Public opinion can affect environmental issues. It can generate support for particular concerns and put political pressure on local and national governments. Many surveys have been carried out on people's attitudes to the environment. A major survey carried out between 1981 and 1984 in the USA, Japan and Europe indicated strong public support for environmental improvement. Oil spillages, air and water pollution, and nuclear and industrial waste disposal were areas of great concern.

Politics and legislation

Politicians and governments are becoming aware of public opinion on environmental issues and of the threat to the world environment. Many countries now have pollution control laws and programmes to encourage waste recycling.

In 1987 the European Economic Community Environment Commission approved a five-year action plan which includes environmental protection in all economic and social policies. The following year a strict pollution law, Proposition 65, was approved in California, USA by a large majority of Californians. The law aims to reduce threats to health from pesticides, toxic wastes and other hazardous material.

The United Nations Environment Programme (UNEP) was established in 1972 to 'keep under review the world environmental situation in order to ensure that emerging environmental problems of wide international significance receive appropriate and adequate consideration by governments'. Each year UNEP issues a report on the state of the world environment. It also has a databank on hazardous chemicals and working groups concerned with the transport, handling and disposal of hazardous wastes.

The European Community has introduced high standards of cleanliness for European beaches. Many fall below the standards, like this polluted beach at Cherville, France.

Encouragement from industry

Industries too are becoming more environmentally responsible as environmental issues hit the headlines.

One of the most well-known industrial programmes for reducing waste at source is the Pollution Prevention Pays (3P) Principle introduced in 1975 by the American corporation 3M. The programme looks for ways of saving money by reducing or re-using waste materials and it is supported by staff training and financial bonus schemes. 3M found that the 3P Principle not only helped the environment, but also saved the company a lot of money in energy and running costs.

More recently, the multinational Dow Chemical Company launched its 'Waste Reduction Always Pays' (WRAP) programme to reduce waste entering the environment. Dow says 'Waste reduction plays a crucial role in environmental protection and in the long-term growth of our business'.

What you can do

'The global stage is set for positive environmental action, which has never been more needed.' UNEP

It's your world that needs help, so what can you do? There are lots of simple practical ways you can help protect the environment. For example, look at what you throw away each day. How can you reduce the amount of the things you throw away? What can be re-used or recycled? Listed below are some suggestions that will help you to reduce waste and recycle it, wherever possible.

Many towns have centres where waste paper, metal and glass can be taken for recycling.

Reducing waste

- *Don't accept an extra paper or plastic bag in shops if you're only going to throw it away.*

- *Write on both sides of paper; use recycled paper products when you can.*

- *Buy drinks in returnable bottles whenever possible.*

- *Avoid buying over-packaged goods.*

- *Are your eyes bigger than your belly? Don't take more food than you can eat!*

- *Save energy – switch off lights and heaters in rooms not being used; wear an extra sweater rather than turn up the heating.*

- *Use your legs – walk or cycle when you can, rather than persuade someone to drive you.*

- *Don't drop litter.*

Re-using and recycling

- *Clothes you have finished with can be passed on or given to charity sales.*

- *Old toys, books and games will be useful to someone else when you have finished with them, so don't throw them away.*

- *Waste paper – find out if there are any waste paper collections organized by your local authority or charities.*

- *Cans – use a tin bank if you have one in your area but wash and squash the tins first.*

- *Bottles and glass – buy returnable bottles when you can; take used glass to the bottle bank. If there are no tin or bottle banks in your area, how about writing to the local authority and asking for one?*

- *Make sure food waste goes on to the compost heap if you have one.*

Learning more

Find out what effect you, and those around you, have on the environment. Different people have different views on environmental issues – find out what they think about waste and recycling and why. There are lots of other books and magazines, as well as television and radio programmes on the subject. Don't keep all this valuable information to yourself – tell other people!

Monitoring

Find out what happens to the waste in your house – where does it go? You can write to your local authority to find out. Look out for obvious signs of illegal waste dumping or polluted land, rivers or air. If you think an individual or organization is behaving irresponsibly towards the environment, you could contact your local newspaper, councillor or MP.

Support a campaign

There are many organizations campaigning for a cleaner, healthier environment and they need members to support them. They can also provide you with information and newsletters. A list of organizations is given on page 46.

*You can help by learning more about environmental issues (**above**). Practical help is also needed, for example cleaning birds*

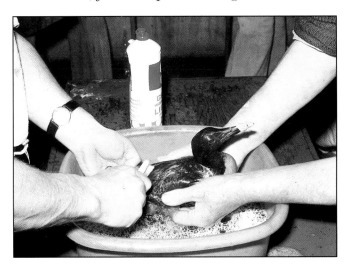

The Bellarmine Beasties

The Bellarmine Beasties is a club run at the Bellarmine Environmental Resource Centre in Pollock in Scotland. In 1987, twenty-five members of the Beasties ran an environmental improvement project in their lunch hours, after school and sometimes at the weekend or on school holidays.

They wanted to clean up the area around their schools and they cleared litter from the playground, a local footpath and a local waterway. They also wanted the local people to be more aware of litter and waste dumping in the area, so they promoted anti-litter messages by producing posters, exhibitions, leaflets and a video featuring an interview with a Coke can!

The Beasties are enthusiastic about their project and they've won several national competitions for their hard work and ideas. Their message to the people of Pollock is 'Keep your city in trim, dispose of litter properly in the bin'.

Glossary

Acid rain Rain, snow, mist or hail which is made more acid by waste gases (sulphur dioxide and nitrogen oxide) discharged into the air.

Arable farming The farming of plant crops such as wheat, barley and vegetables.

Atmosphere The layer of gases surrounding the earth.

Biodegradable The term given to a substance which can be broken down by the natural processes of decomposition.

Conservation The protection and careful use of resources and the environment.

Decompose To break down dead material, putting nutrients back into the environment.

Element A simple substance composed of atoms.

Environment The surroundings or the world that humans and all other animals and plants live in.

Ground water Water held in underground rocks and soil.

Habitat An area in which plants and animals live.

Humus Decomposed plant and animal material that is part of the soil.

Intensive farming Farming which uses high levels of machinery, equipment and fertilizers to operate, usually in a small area of land. Livestock kept in these conditions are said to be factory farmed.

Landfill site A place where solid waste is disposed of, usually a hole in the ground.

Marine pollution The pollution of the seas and oceans.

Micro-organism A living animal or plant which is not visible to the naked eye.

Nutrients The materials which are necessary for growth and life, such as water, minerals, fats and carbohydrates.

Organic waste Waste derived from animal or plant materials.

Pesticide A chemical used to kill plant pests such as aphids and slugs.

Pollution Damage caused to the environment by substances released into it. These substances are known as pollutants.

Radiation The emission, or giving out, of rays, particles or waves by a substance.

Radioactive A radioactive substance is an element which breaks down into another element, at the same time giving out harmful radiation.

Reclamation Saving a waste product so that it can be re-used.

Recycling The processing of waste products for re-use.

Refuse Something which is thrown away.

Resource Anything which is useful to living animals and plants.

Sewage The waste products and water, from homes and from industry, that are flushed down the sink, drain or toilet.

Smog A fog containing human-made pollutants.

Species A group of animals or plants which are capable of breeding with one another.

Toxic waste Waste products that are poisonous.

Unmonitored Without being checked by experts.

Urbanization The making of country areas into cities (urban areas).

Waste Something left over or not used.

Further reading

Air Ecology, Jennifer Cochrane (Wayland, 1987)

A Cleaner World Sarah Allen (Dinosaur/Cambridge
   University Press, 1982)

The Dying Sea, Michael Bright (Franklin Watts, 1988)

The Environment, Adam Markham (Wayland, 1988)

The Junk Book, Bob Graham (Blandford, 1986)

Land Ecology, Jennifer Cochrane (Wayland, 1987)

Looking at Pollution (Batsford, 1986)

Pollution, Michael Gittins/National Society For
   Clean Air (1983)

Pollution and Conservation, Investigating series
   (Arnold Wheaton, 1985)

Recycling – a practical guide for local groups
   (NCVO, 1988)

Toxic Waste and Recycling, Nigel Hawkes (Franklin
   Watts, 1988)

Waste Disposal, Constance Milburn (Blackie, 1985)

Water Ecology, Jennifer Cochrane (Wayland, 1987)

Picture acknowledgements

The publishers would like to thank the following for allowing their photographs to be reproduced in this book:
Bruce Coleman Ltd 9 (NASA), 22 (Norman Myers), 23 above (Norman Tomalin), 24 (Robert Carr), 34 below (Jeff
Foott), 37 below; Frank Spooner Pictures 4 (Stefano Nicozzi), 15 (Eric Bouvet), 20 (Gilbert Uzan), 32; Greenpeace
5, 19, 23 below, 31, 34 above; Hutchison Library 12 (Michael MacIntyre), 23 (Lyn Gambles), 37 above; Oxford
Scientific Films 7 below (Jack Dermio), 8 (Richard Kulah), 22 centre (Sean Morris), 25 above (Jack Dermio); Photri
cover, 7 above, 14 both, 42; Rex Features 16, 17 below, 21 above and below, 33 above and below, 35, 40; Royal
Society for the Protection of Birds 43 (M W Richards); Topham Picture Library 17 above, 27, 29 below, 39, 41; J
M Wycherley 38; ZEFA 18, 36 (Deuter). The artwork is by Stephen Wheele.

Useful addresses

British Scrap Federation
16 High Street
Huntingdon
PE18 8TU

Council for Environmental Education
School of Education
University of Reading
London Road
Reading RG1 5AQ

Friends of the Earth (UK)
26 - 28 Underwood Street
London N1 7JQ

Greenpeace (UK)
30-31 Islington Street
London N1 8XE

Nirex Information Office
Curie Avenue
Harwell
Didcot
Oxon OX11 0RH

Tidy Britain Group
The Pier
Wigan WN3 4EX
(This organization produces Litter Kits)

United Kingdom Atomic Energy Authority
Information Services Branch
11 Charles II Street
London SW1Y 4QP

Waste Watch
NCVO
26 Bedford Square
London WC1B 3HU

Australian Association
for Environmental Education
GPO Box 112
Canberra ACT 2601

Greenpeace (Australia)
310 Angas Street
Adelaide 5000

Friends of the Earth (Australia)
National Liaison Office
366 Smith Street
Collingwood
Victoria 3065

Friends of the Earth (Canada)
Suite 53
54 Queen Street
Ottawa KP5CS

Greenpeace (Canada)
427 Bloor Street West
Toronto
Ontario

Friends of the Earth (New Zealand)
Nagal House
Courthouse Lane
PO Box 39/065
Auckland West

Greenpeace (New Zealand)
Private Bag
Wellesley Street
Auckland

Index